To Lois

SPRING

A THERAPEUTIC RELATIONSHIP

By Leonard Smucker

HERALD PRESS, SCOTTDALE, PENNSYLVANIA

SPRING

Although pseudonyms are used in the manuscript,
permission for its publication has been granted
by the real persons involved.

INTRODUCTION

Dear Len,

There is no full and genuine way for me to convey the range of feelings I encountered in *Spring*, in so many regions of the heart. There were times when I keenly felt your exhilaration, when life seemed at a peak, when at last you had achieved a moment of glory. Then just as suddenly your world collapsed and you had to accept broken pieces and go on again. Who could remain whole in the face of such disillusion and despair? How could trust have any meaning at all, shattered again and again by hypocrisy and lies?

Yes, you became vindictive and suspicious and afraid; you created rules; you even took life in your own hands and ruled by virtue of power and status. But all the way through you remained human; you continued to breathe life in the face of death; you continued to struggle when you were utterly alone and defeated and helpless. And if you were frail at times and caught up in the evil, your senses were rooted in higher ideals and values and your sights were set on an unreachable heaven.

Perhaps it is your willingness to be honest with yourself, however ugly the thoughts, however painful the awareness, which made your encounter with Mary Louise such an all-encompassing human enterprise. Of course, you were often in the dark, steeped in a black pit, but it was the only way to live with her, to relate to her, the only way to discover a direction and crawl back into the light. Perhaps your suffering with her was a more powerful ingredient than love, for you experienced torment and suffering unconditionally with Mary while love had to checked and held in reserve.

It takes courage to live with such an experience and perhaps more courage to share it with others, as openly and as honestly as you have. In the end, you transcended the horror and created new facets of your own identity, and new beauty in gentle, poetic ways, in a realm where most psychotherapists fear to tread.

Thank you for letting me take the powerful journey with you, on return.

Clark
(Dr. Clark Moustakas)
Merrill Palmer Institute of Human Development and Family Life
71 East Ferry Avenue
Detroit, Michigan 48202

1

The privilege of communing with another, of entering intimately into the life of another, of being in touch with another's soul, of knowing another in a deep and fundamental sense, is a sacred and holy honor.

Some experiences cannot be contained. They must be shared. Not for the purpose of winning sympathy or eliciting praise, not to "build a case," not to win support for a cause, not to defend or prove something, not to win converts, but simply because some experiences cannot be contained—they overflow.

This is an experience that opened up my depths, shook my foundations, moved me deeply, awakened within me powerful surges of feeling: of fear, of love, of bitterness, of anger. It has brought me into a more profound sense of life—of the real and the false, of loving and hating, of living and dying, of meeting and parting.

❊   ❊   ❊

She seemed extremely tense and frightened in our first meeting.

"I have a terrible fear of fire," she said. "I wake up thinking I see flames on the wall. Several times I have screamed out. It started when my husband and I were stationed in the Philippines. I have sat up until 3:00 and 4:00 at night fearing sleep and fire. I went down to 96 pounds. . . .I have terrible pains in my stomach. . . . My husband always hits me in the stomach or head. . . . He was kicked out of the Navy for indecent exposure. . . . I'm afraid of people. I don't like them. I tend to be impulsive. When I want to do something I do it—sometimes without thinking. Saturday I had a fight with my husband. I went out driving and hit a tree. A few nights before that the police

8

came to the house, having been told that I had taken too many sleeping pills."

For a period of several months she and I were engaged in an unspoken struggle. I had sensed keenly her fears, her loneliness, her desperation, her despair and felt somehow that if she could trust our relationship, if she could continue regular meetings, something positive could emerge. Although she was carrying an enormously heavy burden, too much for one to bear alone, she seemed to be fighting desperately against committing herself to such a relationship. I knew almost from the first that in spite of her intense turmoil, her crumbling world, I had a kind of faith in the creative possibilities of our meetings.

It was extremely difficult for her to surrender, to let go, to give up and face herself. On several occasions she would leave early before the allotted time had transpired. Sometimes she would become angry and suddenly stalk out. I seldom knew from one time to the next whether she would return. On another occasion she came to the Center without an appointment sobbing painfully, uttering, "I can't go on. I can't stand it anymore. I can't go home. . . . I JUST CAN'T!"

She spoke of a deep craving for affection. She feared that she could not trust herself with men. In her own way she cried out for love and intimacy. She felt it was impossible for anyone to care for her except, perhaps, out of pity.

At times she would feel very strongly that it was not worth going on—that it was hopeless. It was better not to have hope, for hope only nourished more intense anguish and pain. She had suffered many losses in her young life including the death of Jimmy, her son.

"I don't know what I believe; I don't know why I go on at all." She hated her work and yet feared quitting because of the financial crisis they would have to face—a crisis she had faced before.

"I can't go through it again. I just can't," she wailed.

Four months after our first meeting she came in.

"I'm going to say a lot of things and then I'm going to leave and I won't be coming back." She remained standing, went over to the window, and began: "I'm going to be quitting my job in two weeks. I can't stand it any longer. We're going down for the third time. Don talked about filing bankruptcy. I can't lose everything again. I would rather die than lose something else. I remember how it was the last time. We had only a few days' notice. It soon got around that my husband had exposed himself. The people were cruel and mean. They were laughing at us, mocking us, making fun of us as I was packing. I could take along only what could go on the plane—all the rest of our things we had to leave behind. I had to put some of Tommy's favorite toys in the trash. Later, I saw some other children picking them out—things that were Tommy's. It was horrible.

"I'm not going to care now. I am going to do bad things. I want to feel like a woman and I'm going to. No one can convince me otherwise. I'm tired. I can get what I want by stepping on people, by using them."

"I admire your spunk," I said, "your ability to stand up to me. I see a lot of courage and strength in you that could be used constructively."

"Well, you are the only person I've been able to stand up to. I guess I really am going nuts to think that way, but I could go on talking and it wouldn't do any good. I'd be wasting your time."

Then she was gone.

Several weeks later she called me early one morning and asked for an appointment. She stated that she had been driving around for some time and had nearly hit the "jackpot." An appointment was made.

"I can't stop lying. I want to tell you the truth, Jimmy may have been John's baby. I don't know about Tommy. I had been going out with Jerry. I lied about my husband. The reason he hasn't come to see you is because I didn't want him to. I lie; I'm vicious, I keep hurting Don. I feel better when he hits me. I like to make him angry. Compared to me he is a saint. I don't want him to put up with so much. Why does he? The nicer he is to me, the more I hate him. I haven't been a good wife and mother. I've cheated Don and Tommy. I haven't read a book to him for a long time. I'm just an it. I had an operation so I can't have any more babies. I want another one so bad.

"I didn't want to start coming here for fear this would happen. It's like—it's like—I have found some security with you. I'm afraid not to come. I'm afraid I will begin liking you too much. I want you to say, Don't come back. Work it out yourself. I don't know if I want to change and no one can make me. I'd like just to walk out—go somewhere and forget everything."

A day or so later I was interrupted in the middle of an appointment. She sounded desperate.

"I know if I get into the car now I will leave for sure." She sounded as though she wanted me to stop her in some way.

I told her not to get into her car for a while. "Take a walk and then come to the Center. I will meet with you at 5:15."

She continued to convey a feeling of desperation for several moments and then hung up. She did not arrive at the time I had suggested. I waited. Then, just as I was leaving, I was notified that she was in the waiting room.

She looked frightened and dazed. She had that hard, piercing look that I had come to know as a combination of fear, anger, and hopelessness. She sat down and began: "Please tell Don that I'm leaving. Tell him that he can find the car at the bus station in Elmstown. Tell him that I'm no good for anyone and that I have to leave. They will be better off without me. I'm neither a good wife nor mother. I'm vicious. I've lied all my life. I've got to go. There is no other way."

I told her that I felt she had already made a new beginning by sharing with me the truth about herself. If she left now, it would only make it that much harder the next time—that she could not really find what she sought by leaving, for she was running from herself.

She screamed back, "But can't you see? I can't change. I can't. I CAN'T." She looked away and began crying softly. There was a long pause.

I said, "Maybe you are right. Maybe you can't change . . . but I wish you could give yourself another chance."

She gave me that terribly hard piercing look and cried out, "I know what I want and I'm going to get it one way or another. I don't care what anyone thinks. I'm going to get what I want if it's the last thing I do." There was again a pause. She got up to leave. I called her back.

"Please sit down." She remained standing, facing the door. Slowly she turned and sat down. "Before you go I want you to take something with you."

13

I handed her the story of an old man. "This is an experience of a friend of mine, a 74-year-old man who changed . . . you are 26. You can also change if you want to badly enough." I told her with a deep sense of commitment that I would be holding her next appointment open for her. If she didn't come, I would be with her that hour wherever she was. She understood what I meant. She put the paper in her purse.

"Now may I go?"

"Yes."

She left without looking back.

I remained seated at my desk. A flood of thoughts rushed through my mind. Should I try to stop her in some way or should I let her go? Should I inform her husband as she had requested or should I wait? She might return . . . but then again. . . .

I decided to wait, at least for a while, even though that was the most difficult choice. My thoughts continued to be with her—wondering, hoping, fearing.

Then, several hours later, I received a call. She had already traveled some distance.

"I read that paper you gave me. I want to go to the hospital."

Immediately I felt a sense of relief. I told her that I would make arrangements for her to be admitted. "You may enter the hospital through either the front or the back door. Go to the admitting desk and give them your name. They will admit you to the psychiatric ward."

"Will I be going alone?"

"Would you like for me to meet you there?"

"Oh, no, you won't need to."

"I'll meet you there at 10:00."

I waited in the lounge in such a way that I could see her if she entered either door. I tried to hide my nervousness. I looked at several magazines but saw only my thoughts reflected. It was 10:30. Then I heard her walk. She saw me through the window and paused at the door. I could see her eyes search mine quickly. I took her luggage and we went to the desk. She was being asked the routine questions. At one point she turned to me and whispered, "That's twice that I've lied."

The next day was Saturday. About 3:00 in the afternoon I received a phone call.

"I've just taken all the pills that I have."

She had been released from the hospital without my knowledge. I was dumbfounded.

"This time I mean it." She burst into sobs. "I only wanted you to hold me . . . just once . . . was that too much to ask? Just to know that someone really cared?"

"No, that doesn't sound like too much to ask, but I think you must know how much I do care."

The sobbing continued—wailing, gasping sobs. "Oh! My stomach!" She hung up.

I tried calling three different doctors in her home community. No luck. Then I called a Dr. Franklin.

"Is Dr. Franklin there?"

"No, he isn't."

"This is Dr. Smucker and it's important that I reach him."

His wife laughed. "Oh! He's sitting right here."

Would he go and make a home call? Yes, he knew her. He had given her some pills. When he learned of the circumstances, he said, "No, I don't want to become involved."

I finally reached another doctor who was on a home visit at the time.

Dr. White called back sometime later. She had taken a pretty stiff dose, "but I think she'll make it all right. She was sitting on the couch with her husband when I left."

Another call two hours later. It was Dr. White. "This is the next chapter on Mrs. Rogers. She just slashed her wrists and was brought to the hospital in an ambulance. What should I do now?"

"She should be returned to the psychiatric ward in the city hospital near the Center. I will make arrangements and you can have them go directly to the hospital."

Another phone call. It was Mr. Rogers. "Are the arrangements made?"

"Yes."

"She wants to know when she can see you."

"I will see her at the hospital tonight."

She saw me as I arrived on the ward. We exchanged searching glances. I finally started. "I was glad you could tell me what you did over the phone." She said that her "imagination" was making her "half crazy." She pleaded with me to hold her just once "to stop my imagination."

I told her that I could understand her longing for closeness but that I would not hold her. That was not my way.

Her whole body shook with hate and anger. There was that terrible look of resentment and defiance in her eyes. "I don't care how long you keep me here," she screamed; "when I get out I'll kill myself, I WILL. . . ." She looked powerful enough to tear me to shreds. She jerked open her purse and held out the paper in an attempt to return it. I knew what she was saying—"I'm not going to try again for anyone." She held it out for a long time, staring at me with piercing eyes. Finally with great reluctance I took the paper. I asked her gently, "Why must you fight so? Why must you be so hard and cold? You must know that you cannot bargain with someone for a relationship."

"I'm not bargaining," she snapped back.

"But you've said you will kill yourself unless I hold you."

Her expression changed. She began to melt. "Can't you see? . . . I'm no good to anyone. I'm

17

no good . . . I'M NO GOOD. . . . I have nothing to give to others. I can't love anyone but myself."

A few moments later she looked up at me and said, "I was just thinking. Maybe you're the one who is cold."

"Perhaps to you I am in a physical way because I will not hold you, but I have a pretty tender heart."

She relaxed and smiled. "I know you do. You are so—so—caring. I've never met anyone like you."

"Then you do know that I care?"

"Yes." She reached out her hand once more for me to return the paper. "I knew it when I was talking about Tommy and you said—you said—" She looked away and could not finish. I knew what she meant. I had said that when she talked that way about Tommy, how she had neglected him and cheated him, I wanted to cry with her.

In those next moments words and feelings mingled as we discovered each other beyond the stereotypes of "doctor" and "patient"—stereotypes to which we too often cling out of fear and distrust of ourselves and the other.

"You must have an extraordinary wife."

"Yes, I do," I said simply. "However, we are people. We have our highs and our lows."

"Does everyone have feelings like that?"

"Yes."

She looked at me in earnest, "You're not lying?"

"No."

"What do you do when you feel sad?"

"Sometimes I take a walk, I write, or I talk with a friend. Not too long ago I climbed to the top of a high tree. I felt very sad and alone. From the top of the tree I could hear someone laughing. I saw a little church in the distance. I saw the beauty of a newly formed leaf."

Suddenly I realized that I was sharing something that perhaps had personal meaning only for me. I laughed self-consciously. "It would probably seem silly to some if they had seen me in the tree."

"No," she said, "I can understand." And with a faraway look she continued, "I used to crawl on top of our chicken house and just be alone for a while."

Once more she talked about the "torturing thoughts" she had about me. "I know it's bad to have those thoughts. . . . They hurt too much."

"How do you mean 'it's bad to have such thoughts'?"

She paused for several moments, then revealed her thoughts in frank, spontaneous resignation. "Well, I guess if I half love you I half love you . . . there's nothing I can do about it."

"If you can come to honestly love one person, then you can come to love others as well. You do have something to give to others. You have given me a great deal just now. You have let me know you—your real feelings. You have let me see your heart. You have shared with me something deep inside you."

She was radiant when I left. I was bursting with emotion. I wanted to cry and laugh at the same time. I felt close to the whole world. I gave a special good-night kiss to each of our four boys.

Four-year-old Stanford looked up at me with hopeful questioning eyes, "Is she going to get better?"

"Yes."

He clutched his pillow fondly, smiled with joy, and exuded a sweet kind of peace.

I relived the experience with my wife as we sipped tea and watched the rain come down in torrents outside our picture window. It was swirling the leaves, washing them, cleansing them in an almost violent sort of way. I was tired and at peace.

2

When her family learned of her hospitalization and the cutting of her wrists, they came from a distant state to be with her. I soon found out that her parents and sister never knew for sure if they could trust Mary. They told of times when she would suddenly take Tommy, board a bus, and leave for a period of time, of her temper, of her lies, her "tricks," her addiction to pills, of how she always wanted the best of everything and got it one way or another. They suspected that she may have cut her wrists in order to have them come to her rescue financially.

I recall the family session vividly. She was seated on a couch with her mother on one side and her sister on the other. Her husband was present, his mother and sister.

Her father began, "I told the others I was going to say this, and I'm going to come right out and say it. I've been thinking that this might be another one of your tricks." He turned toward her, held her gaze, and dared to raise the direct question, "IS THIS A TRICK?"

Mary sounded pained and hurt, "No! No! No!"

She started sobbing and ran out of the room. Her sister and mother left to follow in an attempt to console her. I found the three of them some distance down the hall. I asked the mother and sister to return to the room. I stood by her while she cried quietly—her head and arms against the wall.

"How much more of this do I have to take?"

"I don't know, but I want you to return to the room with me."

She turned slowly and started back. She was frightened and shaky. After we were seated once more, I began, "Mary feels that no one believes she is sincere."

There was a pause, then a number of superficial attempts to express belief in her. Her father clutched the arms of his chair hard—looked straight at her and with choked emotion continued, "Mary, I believe you. I don't know for sure, but I have faith in you. I may be wrong, but I'm willing to put my faith in you."

Don, on the verge of tears, "I want to do anything I can to keep my family together for the sake of Tommy."

° ° °

Mary remained at the Center for a number of days. Sometimes she would sit by herself or stare mournfully out of the window.

"I'm numb. . . . I don't have feelings anymore. I am afraid of what might happen when I have feelings again."

Several times she remarked that perhaps, after all, it had been only a trick—as though she had no way of knowing anything with certainty. Gradually, over a period of time, she was able to rejoin her husband and son at home.

Then one morning she called for an appointment. "I want now to tell all."

She came in carrying a sealed envelope. She was trembling as she handed it to me. "Here. I've written it. I don't want to be here when you open it."

She started to leave. I took her arm gently and told her that I would prefer that she remain with me while I read it. She hesitated and then sat down, doubled up in the chair. She began crying in aching sobs. Her whole body convulsed with terrible paroxysmal weeping. I read the note and pondered it for several moments. It was very short, only three lines. It read:

"For four years I've tried to convince myself that I had nothing to do with Jimmy's death. He's dead because I killed him. I want my punishment."

I was frozen by its contents. I could not speak.

"Go ahead," she screamed. "Call the police. I don't care anymore, I don't care what happens now. . . . SAY SOMETHING!"

She held her hands to her face. Her whole body wreathed sobs of agony. She suddenly ripped off a necklace she had always worn and threw it violently across the room. It was a plain necklace with a single silver cross.

It was some time before I could speak. "It's a terrible thing to take the life of another." Again there was silence. Then words began to come, "Perhaps—perhaps you have already experienced a more cruel punishment than any man could devise for you—four years of trying to live with this burden by yourself. What worse torture, what greater hell, than to live alone with the knowledge of having killed your own son."

She stood up, tried to run out of the room, but I could not let her go. I held her while she continued to struggle—finally falling limp at my feet. A little later she was able to return to her chair. She began to relax slightly.

I had an appointment to meet with both of them late that afternoon.

"I could never tell him," she said.

"Would you like to try?"

She wanted to but was afraid it would only make their relationship more intolerable. Finally she said with courage, "I will try. I want to go home now, but I will be back later with Don."

I was amazed at her strength to continue.

I kept reliving that hour with her so vividly that I could not honestly give myself to meet the other appointments of the day. I had a stronge urge to be with her—to share her suffering. Some time later I called and asked if she would permit me to come and be with her for a time.

It was raining. Several times I started to go and then turned back as I thought of all the usual reasons why I should not heed such an impulse. Didn't I have a responsibility to meet the appointments already scheduled? How would such action be viewed in the light of my "professional role"? Would I be jeopardizing my own position or the positions of those with whom I worked? Could she possibly understand and accept my wish to be with her? Although I was able to raise a staggering number of questions, somehow it seemed that the only honest action for me at that moment was to go—not so much for her as for myself.

When I arrived, she opened the door and invited me to come in. She had been sitting quietly in a darkened room looking through the baby books of Tommy and Jimmy. I wanted her to understand that I came not so much for her but because I felt I wanted to be with her. I wanted to share what she was going through. To my surprise she seemed to understand. I sat across the room from her. Her hands were clasped together, her head bowed. There was a knowing silence. After a few moments she asked if I would like to look through the baby books.

I looked through Tommy's first. She had written in it precious little sayings and experiences through the years of Tommy's young life. Then I turned to Jimmy's. He had been born on Halloween. The pictures and notations reflected his mother's obvious pride. The book came to an abrupt ending as had his life—never to be completed.

The knowing silence continued. The tears between us were many. I thanked her for permitting me to come. I felt that I could again return to the Center.

Rather than wait alone for Don to come, she decided to accompany me back to the Center and wait for him there. It was still raining.

With the windshield wiper's steady drone in the background she told me the details of Jimmy's death. He had been playing in his playpen near the fireplace. As her husband was aboard ship, she was alone much of the time with all of the responsibilities of a young child. Jimmy cried a great deal. She had noticed that there were some bugs that had come in around the fireplace. She went to get some spray. Jimmy was crying again. Suddenly on impulse she turned on Jimmy with the insect spray and sprayed and sprayed. "I couldn't stop. I saw him sink to the floor, his eyes looking up at me. He began to change color. I took him to the Navy hospital. They took all kinds of tests. Hours later the doctor came out and told me that he had died and that his death was due to a gastrointestinal disorder."

We reached the Center. As we got out of the car, she looked up at me and said, "I hope you will never be sorry that you came this afternoon."

"No," I said after considering it a moment, "I don't think I shall ever be sorry."

She had asked me to tell her husband everything first and then to have her come in later. "I couldn't stand to see the look on his face when he is told," she said.

He was there promptly for the 4:00 appointment. There was something remarkable about this young man. In fact, there was something very remarkable about both of these young people. In my previous contacts with him I felt somehow that he would stand by her. He had said, "After all, my record is far from spotless."

It did seem that they knew how to hurt each other cruelly and were capable of destroying each other emotionally, but there seemed to be something else that bound them together.

He took a chair. I closed the door. It was hard for him to accept. He had heard the doctor's report. They had thought for some time that the baby may not have "been right." He could hardly crawl or sit up at a year and a half. He was always crying. I told him that she had been trying for four years to live with this haunting memory and that it was a terribly difficult experience for her to share with anyone.

He said he was ready to be with her. He walked up to her, took her hand, and together they walked back to my office. They both met that hour with courage. I watched them leave—together—and then sank back into my chair alone. All the events of that day kept tumbling around in my mind.

I entertained the hope that perhaps now this couple could begin their life together anew, that perhaps their life and lot would begin to improve.

3

Sometime later she came in for her appointment but remained standing. She began haltingly. "Don was told last night that he would be laid off work tonight. It's all my fault. I can't take it anymore. Last night I couldn't sleep . . . the details of Jimmy's death keep going through my mind. I must really be cracking up. I could smell the flowers at his funeral. Please don't let me be afraid again."

She looked desperate. "Can't you take the memories away? Can't you give me shock treatments? Isn't that supposed to close off your memory?"

I could not recommend shock treatment. "It might erase memories for a while but in the end it would only prolong the hell."

"Can't you do something?"

"I'm afraid not. It is something you will have to live with."

"No! No!" she shouted. "I can't—I can't—I CAN'T TAKE IT."

She began walking to the door. I got there first and stood firm. "Please sit down." She suddenly whirled around.

"All right! We have 17 minutes. Start talking!"

"I can't tell you what to do. I thought together we could find some way out—some answer."

"There isn't any now. Thanks for all you've done, but it's no use anymore. I can't go on living this way. I don't want you to give me any more false hopes. Let me go. You'll have to let me go in seven minutes."

"Yes, I know."

Then she stated, "I was going to go and try to find something."

"What do you mean?"

"You'd laugh."

"No, I wouldn't."

"I want to find a spot—a spot by a river and sit for a while. I don't know why, but I did that once when I was nine." Her eyes were misty as she fought to hold back tears.

"I understand."

I stood back. She opened the door and left. I felt she had to find her own way even though I knew she might very well try to take her life once more. I saw her car drive off. I breathed a prayer with my whole being. "God, don't let this girl die." It was the kind of prayer that I had uttered in my youth— an asking, begging prayer. I chastised myself. Intellectually I knew that there was no magical God who would intervene. I felt that there was a fifty-fifty chance that she would make the decision to live. I felt I had to trust her even though it was extremely difficult. After several hours I looked for her car to return. I thought she might call—nothing.

Some time later I received a call from the nurse saying Mary had just returned to the Center and seemed pretty desperate. I went to the room where she was lying down. We searched each other's faces. Our hands went out to each other. She gripped me hard as I held her hand in both of mine.

"Don't ever let me do that again. I can't go on being bounced back and forth this way."

"I'm glad you were able to return."

Soon the grimness broke and she smiled faintly. "I've never had anyone really stay by me this way."

"I intend to continue staying by you, but I am reaching the point where you are going to have to assume more responsibility for yourself. I can't keep second guessing you. I don't know how much more I can go through with you."

She expressed a feeling of being relaxed and of wanting to sleep. I left.

That evening she gave Miriam, the nurse, two small gold rings and a necklace. The rings were the rings Jimmy and Tommy had worn as babies. The necklace was the one she had ripped from her neck during that painful, agonizing confession.

Miriam left me this note:

Mary gave these to me and wanted me to deliver them personally to you, but I had to leave before I could see you. She said to tell you to keep them until she is worthy of them. She wanted you to have them over the weekend and she couldn't see you to do this.

It was during this time, like ripples on a lake, that I felt myself coming to know Miriam and Dick in a more fundamental way. They, too, had come to know Mary and responded to her much as I had. They were among the first that Mary trusted enough to tell of the awful death of Jimmy. Mary's relationships were beginning to spread beyond me at a time when my emotional exhaustion was beginning to tell. I was becoming remote, irritable and edgy at home. I was reaching the bottom of my endurance.

4

Often it seemed that she was testing the strength of our relationship. At times she wanted to make me angry with her so that I would break it off. The relationship meant hope, but for her hope was something to fight against, for it led only to greater hopelessness.

The next time I saw her she entered the room,

closed the door, and remained standing.

"You're going to hate me for this . . . but I've tried everything else." She grabbed me and held me tight against her—her arms around my neck. I could smell a slight tinge of peppermint gum. I didn't move, nor did I push her aside.

"Now you know what I really am. If you would just hate me, it would make it so much easier. I can't change. I'm no good. I can't love. . . . I've never known a friendship like the one you've given me and I don't know how to cope with it. I would much rather that people hated me, then I know where I stand. I have to be hard now because there is no job, no clothes for Tommy. I can't change, I don't want to change. I told you I couldn't keep bouncing back and forth."

"Somehow," I said, "because you have let me know you I can't feel differently toward you. I can't honestly find it within myself to hate you . . . but if continuing to see me is hurting you in some way, then I don't want you to continue. My relationship to you, my feeling about you, does not seem to change. If you have to become hard, if you have to put your armor back on . . . well . . . I wish it could be otherwise, but that's a decision you have to make."

"I've already made it," she snapped. She got up to leave. She had put her armor back on. She had to be hard, insensitive, in order to survive at all. I felt that she had to break with me in order to meet the present crisis even if that meant returning to the old pattern.

I saw her again sometime later. "I'm very sorry for what happened. If you would have pushed me away, I would have left for sure—it would have been easier."

"What did you mean, you don't know how to cope with the feelings of having a friend?"

"Well, it's like when I was in the hospital and I wanted you to hold me and you said no. That had never happened to me before. I thought maybe you weren't human . . . maybe you could help me. Then when I called that time and I heard your wife's voice and the children in the background, I began to see you as human. Like when my sister said Daddy isn't a god. I felt then that you couldn't help me anymore."

"You mean you were disappointed in me?"

"Yes. Now it seems I'm just back where I started. What is the use of continuing to meet with you? What good would it do to tell you how I feel?"

"I've been human all the time, but you have just discovered it now. To me, that is a kind of compliment; to you it's a disappointment."

She gave me that cold, hard stare, then left as though she would never return again.

° ° °

When I am at a low ebb, I often walk through the woods at night. I had been doing this frequently as I neared the depths of my own resources. I walked this night and then put my thoughts in these words:

Something in me has been shattered. This whole experience with her has shaken my foundations, my faith in myself, in others, in the value of love. Sometimes I feel that I have so much love bottled up in me somewhere waiting for a "yes" that will respond in the same key. I was honest, I was genuine, I loved, I was open with another. . . . I shared myself and the pain and suffering of the other. It was not enough. . . . I know that being human as I was with the other was somehow right for me. It was me in a very real way and yet the other was left confused, disappointed, angry with me for not hating her, for not severing the bond that had grown between us. She had to sever it for some reason not wholly clear to me so that she could leave and build on her own strength or return to a deceptive life. She was familiar with hate—when someone loved, it left her angry, disappointed, wanting to destroy the relationship. I could not honestly find it within myself to hate her and that only increased her pain. My regard for her was hurting her, was driving her more and more back to the familiarly deceptive ways.

This has been a deeply humbling experience. One that has left me pained and hurt. What can I believe in? I have always thought and felt that love of a healthy and genuine kind was a curative force . . .

now I know that it can produce pain and suffering—
that it can drive a person into a hard shell; it can
destroy.

I suppose that I like to think that what happened
just now is only temporary, that eventually from this
experience I will see that my belief is confirmed, but
I don't know and can't know if that will ever happen.

I wept as I told my wife of my broken spirit, of
my foundations being shaken, of a deep sense of
lostness. There was something strangely restorative in
that precious experience with my wife.

There were other times when I knew what it was
to feel alone with my thoughts—terribly alone—
and yet at the same time knowing that I had to
be again in touch with myself, my own soul, before I could relate meaningfully to another. The following poem grew out of an intense experience of
being alone, lost, out of touch.

I walked the lonely night air.
The trees, their leaves stilled, were there to comfort me,
But they could not touch my heavy soul.
I longed for a silent, knowing friend to walk with me
Who understood my longings,
But there was no one—
Only the trees, the stars, and the lonely path.

I wanted to be in touch with another whose soul
    knew the ache of heaviness.
I cried out to the other in the dark night, but
    there was no answer—

Only the quiet leaves responding to an occasional
    breeze.
What is this dark gnawing of my depths, this quiet
    bleeding?
I want to commune with the depths of another, but
    there is no other—
Only bursting, crying, aching, longing within.
Only me . . . alone. . . .
ME!

5

Sometime later I was interrupted during an appointment. It was a call from my wife. She sounded frantic. "Mary was just here. . . . When I answered the door, she just stood there . . . mumbled her name and stared. Finally she said, 'I just wanted to meet you first. I didn't know there were people like Dr. Smucker, but I guess if there's one, there must be more and my husband can find one . . . but I wanted to meet you first.' I asked her to come in, but she ran to her car and sped away. I don't know what she's going to do. . . ."

I called her husband and told him what happened. At times the only thing that gave me hope was the items she entrusted to me—as though to say, "Someday I will come back. I won't give up."

Hours later there was a call from a gas station. "Are you Mrs. Rogers' doctor?"

"Yes."

"Looks like she took an overdose of sleeping pills. Her wrists look like she may have cut them."

"Bring her to the Center."

She was taken into a small room with a couch. There were no words spoken. She seemed dazed. I sat silently with her in the room. Several times she raised slightly and screamed out, "Jimmy, JIMMY!" All at once she began getting up.

She was half standing, half clinging to the wall. "I want to leave."

"I don't feel you are in a condition to leave at present." I tried to return her to the couch. She sat down for a while. Then she got up, looked at me with terrible anger and hate. "I'm leaving here." I told her once more that I could not let her do that.

"Please try to understand. It is because I care

that I can't allow you to go just now."

"All right, you've asked for it . . ." and her face became tight, her scowl horribly intense. She looked as if she was capable of giving me a terrible battle. I kept hoping someone else would come along, but there was no one around. She began to reach for her high-heeled shoes and I knew from her sister that she had used those spikes very effectively with her father on a previous occasion. I had heard that she could fight like the devil when her temper was aroused. I tried to push the shoes to one side but was unsuccessful. I was relieved when she put them on her feet.

"I'm asking you one more time to let me go. You don't know how I can fight."

She began to come toward me.

"I'm ready," I said.

Although the whole experience seems tinged with humor now, it was a dreadfully grim period. I knew that we had no legal right to forcibly detain her and yet I felt strongly, in view of past experiences with her, that I was doing in fact what she would want me to—to stand by her when she became so angry that she was afraid of what she might do.

Suddenly she stopped. "I can't fight you. You are better and stronger than I am."

She returned to the hospital. Once there, she repeated her earlier threat, "I don't care how long you keep me here, I'll kill myself when I get out."

I felt myself becoming vindictive. I wanted to keep her there for some time so that I wouldn't have to worry from one time to the next what she might do. Like the parents who told me of their boy, "We keep him locked in his room because every time he gets out we worry for fear he'll get in trouble again."

I felt that I wanted to have her confined for a very long time. I was at the end of my strength. I wanted her locked up so that I could get some rest, so that I could regain my own resources. Then I began to realize more clearly than before what I had known intellectually. I could not ultimately assume the responsibility for another human life. The next afternoon I permitted her to return to the Center.

The next few weeks were difficult. Her husband had been offered another job. After terminating the one he had, he discovered that he could not be hired until he had an operation for hernia. He would need to be in the hospital for five or six days and then it would be three or four weeks before he could go to work. They had no hospitalization insurance and no way of paying any of the bills. They had tried in every conceivable way to stall off creditors. They had sold all of their furniture; their phone had been disconnected; there was no money for food. She knew that she had to be strong for him.

6

Then the day came when she asked for the return of the items she had entrusted to me. "I'm ready," she said, simply.

She wanted me so much to understand her feelings. "If I come back, I want all of you and I know I can't have that. Each time I come back it hurts more. I don't want to keep coming and feel that

hurt of never really being a part of you. I've discovered Tommy again. I've been going to the library
and doing some reading. I can't see you anymore—
any of you. I've never known any place like this. I've
never met people like you."

I could feel a kind of pain within, a kind of
sadness, that something beautiful in our relationship
had now to be ended and for the reason that she
wanted it to continue. She "hurt" too much in
coming, nourishing a wish that we could become
more a part of her life and knowing or thinking, at
the same time, that this was not possible. There is
irony in this—that a relationship has to be broken
because of the wish to have it continued.

At such times I loathe boundaries—boundaries of
any kind that separate—whether they be social,
racial, political, religious, or professional. I hate
man's stereotypes, his roles, his categories, his molds,
his prejudices, his culturally induced boundaries and
walls. Why must we both suffer when continuing
the relationship seems so natural—when we could
continue something rich and meaningful to both?

But then I know, too, that men need walls and
boundaries for protection, for survival. Walls are
erected in order to preserve that for which loss is
feared.

We extended our hands to each other. I did not
want to let her go. We held fast. She pulled away
once, but I held firm until I was done with what

I wanted to say. I relaxed my grip and she relaxed hers. Then she was gone.

I continued to ponder the question, "Why can't I be a friend of man and continue meaningful relationships?" Once more I cursed all barriers that separate and leave incomplete. Then I realized that there was a sense of completion. We have lived through the whole gamut of emotions together. We have lived through it together. That has been . . . and will remain forever. Nothing can destroy that—neither man nor culture. It will live and not die.

   o o o

She sometimes spoke of herself, "Mary Louise," as two different persons. The one, "Mary," was cunning, deceptive, cruel, and the other, "Louise," was kind, loving, and unpretentious. Before leaving, she left this note:

I wish I could wrap in a box the Louise of last week and take her home to Don and Tommy for a present. I wish I could give her to everyone that Mary has ever met and hurt. She wasn't just another impression that Mary created. Mary could never behave that well for so many days; also, it was never an enjoyable or particularly happy time when Mary was busy creating a good impression. Louise really enjoyed herself and was as close to being happy as any human can possibly be. . . .

My sister-in-law, my husband, my parents, and everyone else make me feel so guilty. If they only knew how very much I, wanted to be Louise. If they only knew that Louise really exists somewhere inside of Mary. Then maybe they would give me the time I still need. . . .

I carry the letter you gave me and the little story about the old man with me wherever I go. I'll always keep them with me and just hope that maybe someday I'll have another chance. One helps me to have faith in people like you; the other helps me to believe that maybe someday there really will be another me.

. . . Thank you, Dr. Smucker, for helping me to have at least one wonderful week. Thank you for just being you.

I was very much moved by the note, for I knew that I had met Louise—that she did exist "somewhere inside of Mary."

○   ○   ○

Several weeks passed and then one day she made a brief visit to the Center.

"May I ask you a favor? Would you take these things back?"

"I don't understand."

"That way I'll always know when I look for them that this place is here. If those things ever get in your way, you can do whatever you want to with them."

46

She handed me the necklace with the cross and the two tiny gold rings.

Seeing her again, her smile, her honesty, her hard-won victories, was an immense pleasure. It warmed me. I scribbled down my own personal reactions to the experience of that day:

> She is not demanding so much from us. She is living her life more responsibly. I'm no longer so concerned about her, so frightened, so anxious about her. I enjoy very much being with her, but I don't feel responsibility for her. That is the most refreshing, the most freeing, relieved kind of feeling. She has her own strength even though unsteady at times. It is as though she has given me a gift in being more responsible for herself. She no longer has to depend so much on my strength but can call forth her own. There is something equalizing about that. We are both persons who enjoy being with each other but relatively free from possessiveness. Seeing her for a few minutes today made my whole day a joy.

7

One day she called. She implored me to help her break her relationship to the Center and to me. In almost desperate tones she pleaded, "Please, PLEASE help tear me away!"

I told her that if she really felt that she had to sever her relationships completely, if continuing it off and on was crippling her in some way, then I would want her to make an appointment for the purpose of effecting a separation. She wanted time to think it over.

Several days later she requested such an appointment. This was to be our last meeting together by mutual agreement. She had said that this would be a new experience for her. Every previous time she left someone she had to make him mad at her. She didn't know the meaning of parting as friends.

She was dressed attractively but simply. She came quietly to the office and sat down. I began, "We have lived through a great many experiences together and now . . . one of the hardest."

"You know, I didn't know if I could go through with this. I was going to tear up what you had given me and leave it here and walk off."

"I'm glad you decided not to."

We both knew that at 12:00 noon we would part. Time flew rapidly. The experience of our last meeting cannot be described. It was a deeply religious experience. There were tears and smiles, knowing silence and words that flowed out as we relived some of the earlier meetings as well as the present moment.

She had decided that the only way she could effect the separation was to leave this area and return to her home in Kansas.

"I know when I leave here I will have to be Mary again. My folks will have already told the lies to the neighbors about my coming and I will have to go along with it."

"That kind of hurts," I said, "to think that you will have to change back to being Mary."

"I don't want you to be hurt," she said tenderly.

I added quickly, "I can survive that hurt."

Before we knew it the hands of the clock were pointing to 12:00. We both looked at the clock and then stood. She paused a moment at the door, "I'll miss you," she said and then turned and quickly walked down the hall.

I was exhilarated. I could hardly contain my joy and sorrow. I knew that I had somehow been enriched through having known her. My depths had been opened up in a way never before experienced. To have shared a part of her life, no matter how stormy it had been, would stay with me.

At 12:00 that day I knew joy. At 6:30 that evening my joy turned to the most profound bitterness I had ever known. I received a call from Madison, Wisconsin. It was from her sister.

Mary had called her at 12:15, just 15 minutes after leaving my office, and told her in pleading tones that she was about to take an overdose of sleeping pills and this time she really meant it. Mary wanted her sister to come to her rescue by taking Tommy and her—without letting Don know—to Madison where she would live and find a job. Her sister had agreed to meet her at the time designated. Mary told her sister that I had advised her to leave her husband and go to live in Madison.

She had told me that she would have to change back to "Mary," but I had no idea that she would change that quickly—only 15 minutes after she stepped out of my office. I was stunned by the sister's call. I couldn't believe that she could revert so completely to her old tactics. I could feel the terrible hurt and anger inside toward her for the last bit of deception. I felt I had been violated, used, fooled. That now, I, along with all the others, could no longer believe in her. And yet, I knew, too, that this seemed to be the only way in which she could escape her dilemma—for the old ways had served her well in the past. It was out of desperation that she had contrived this new stratagem. I sat for two hours alone, frozen at what had happened. I could feel myself having to erect a wall. I tried to put my reactions into words—feelings that were so much a part of me that night:

> You have betrayed me. Go on, make fools out of people the rest of your life. Use them and their concern and regard for you as a weapon against them. Betray, lie, deceive, trick, that is a pattern that enslaves you. You may achieve certain ends that you so desperately desire . . . and then . . . one day you will discover too late, that you have destroyed yourself and only the duped will mourn your loss.

These were cruel, hateful feelings that flowed out. Somehow I began to realize once again that the reason I felt let down was that she refused to change in a way that I deemed good. Why couldn't I allow her to be "Mary" and still care about her? She had come to me because her way of life had broken down. Through our meetings she had gained the strength to again continue her way of life. I had to face my own conditional love. I loved her on the condition that she would assume responsibility for herself and family, that she would change from lying, deceit, and trickery, to honesty, openness, and genuineness. I wanted to believe that the seeds for a new Mary had been planted—seeds that would make it more difficult for her to live a lie.

After all, she did have the right to choose her own way. This was hard for me to accept, but I found myself not being able to eradicate the rich meaning and value of our relationship. That would live on for me. I knew deep inside that I did not really hate her. In some ways it would have been easier if I could have.

Then weeks later, I received a note that Mary had called from some little town in Kansas. She wanted me to return the call at her expense. I didn't know whether I wanted to answer it or not. I didn't know if I could be involved anymore.

Finally, I decided to return the call. A voice on the other end answered, "Dr. Smucker?"

"Yes."

"Am I breaking all the rules and regulations?"

I said quietly, "Yes."

She was silent.

"Go ahead."

"I told my folks everything. I left there so I could get away from you all. I won't be using you as a crutch anymore. I'm not going to Madison. I will be returning to Don. I just wanted to know that you are still there."

I was surprised that she was planning to return. I wanted to believe that she wouldn't use me as a "crutch" anymore, but I couldn't help feeling that it would likely be otherwise.

I didn't hear from her again until sometime later. She wrote:

Was I kicked out of the Center for good or may I stick my head in someday and tell the others "hello"? Better yet, how will I know if it's permissible or not? We're starting to church Sunday after next. How's that for a starter?

Someday will you explain just exactly what did happen and why I can honestly say now that life is "pretty good"?

Mary

P.S. Absolute truth, so help me.

I wrote the following in reply:

My response to you has been delayed pending the completion of a diabolical project entitled, "Booby

54

Trap." In response to your question as to whether or not you have been "kicked out of the Center," please be duly informed of the following:

There have been planted on these grounds a vast network of booby traps with your name attached. If you should ever so much as set foot in the area, you would be immediately jettisoned into orbit accompanied only by a one-way ticket.

I trust you will consider seriously the hazards of such a visit before placing your life in jeopardy.

Seriously, it was nice to know . . . that life for you is "pretty good." My regards to you, Don, and Tommy.

Her return note was simple. "So maybe I've always been interested in the exploration of outer space."

8

During our last meeting I had told Mary that I wanted to try to capture in words my experience with her. It was near Christmas when I felt moved to write as follows:

I mentioned that I was going to attempt to relive my experience with you in writing in order that I might share it with others. I have completed a rough draft.

My wife and I belong to a small group with whom we meet regularly. We have learned to know and share with each other in some depth. I read the rough draft at our last meeting. There seemed to be rather deep understanding and sensitivity to you and what you have gone through. I did not, of course, reveal anything that would identify you in any way. You can be assured of confidentiality.

We talked about the way in which people in a conforming society fear risking involvement with their "neighbor," how we have become insensitive to our own conscience, particularly in time of war where killing is praised. One of the men in the group slipped away and returned with a book entitled, *Burning Conscience,* by Gunther Anders. He wanted me to read it, as he felt it has some parallels to your own experience.

It is the story of Claude Eatherly, the pilot who flew the lead plane over Hiroshima and gave the go-ahead signal to drop the first A-bomb which killed 200,000 people. He found it terribly difficult to live with himself. He tried in many ways to force society and others to "punish him." He tried to erase the memory through the use of drugs and medication in an attempt to deaden his tremendous feeling of guilt. At night faces and nightmares would torment him. In his dreams he saw the agonized faces of those burning in the hellfire of Hiroshima. He was in a veterans' hospital—considered mentally ill—for six to eight years. The people who praised him as a hero for dropping the bomb turned against him when he began to denounce war and the buildup of arms. . . .

One of the most moving parts of the book was a letter from some Hiroshima girls who had been scarred and maimed for life as a result of the bomb. They wrote:

. . . we heard recently that you have been tormented by a sense of guilt after the Hiroshima incident and that because of it, you have been hospitalized for mental treatment.

This letter comes to you to convey our sincere sympathy with you and to assure you that we now do not harbor any sense of enmity to you personally. . . . We have learned to feel towards you a fellow-feeling, thinking that you are also a victim of war like us.

We wish that you will recover soon completely and decide to join those people who are engaged in the good work to abolish the barbarous thing called 'war' with the spirit of brotherhood" (1, pp. 25, 26).

Eatherly is now free and has dedicated his life to awakening the consciences of others. His own sense of guilt spurred him on to devote his life to exploring the dangers of atomic armaments and to the promotion of brotherhood throughout the world.

After our last group meeting, I began to ponder to myself, "What would Jimmy write to you if he could?" This came out of my "imagination."

Dear Mommy:

I know how you have been tormented by a terrible sense of guilt since the incident that cost me my life. I know how you have wanted to erase the awful memory, how much you have sought relief by pills, by running, by attempting to end your own life. You wanted to be punished, thinking that it would relieve your troubled soul. You made people hate you and hurt you, not knowing just why, but feeling that you didn't deserve to live or to love.

I know, too, that after four years—years of trying to run and escape the memory—you have had the courage to face it squarely yourself and with others.

I do not hold it against you. You have suffered terribly—the flames on the wall, the smell of the flowers, the abdominal pains, the lying and deception both to yourself and to others. Although Daddy seldom shows it, I know how much he has suffered too.

May the memory serve to spur you on to live your life more humanly, without pretension or deception. May you discover ways of promoting life and love wherever you can, realizing that some people who live are dead. Some people have become the masks they have put on and have lost touch with themselves. They need to be awakened to a fuller life of love, beauty, and truth.

It means much to me that you have had the courage to live with your conscience. You don't need to blot it out anymore. I will live on with you. Have courage. Do not be afraid. The spirit of Christmas is upon us.

Please, Mommy, accept my forgiveness.

Love, Jimmy

Two days after Christmas Mary called and asked for an appointment. It was by now a familiar sound —one of intense desperation, a fear of what she might do. This time she wanted to tell me something she hadn't been able to before.

I didn't trust her call. I knew that if an appointment was offered, I would be permitting her to break our parting agreement. On the other hand, she might be in real danger. I thought of the boy who cried "wolf" the third time. I decided to take a chance and give her the benefit of the doubt.

She was trembling when she came in. "No one will believe that I killed Jimmy. I didn't use spray. Anyone would know that was a lie. I gave him oil of wintergreen. I did it deliberately."

"I remember the first thing that Don said when he returned from aboard ship, 'That's a helluva way to get us back together.' "

She recalled the funeral—how her mother had said, "Stop acting that way or people will think you're crazy."

"When I told my parents, they laughed." In agony and desperation she shouted, "NO ONE WILL BELIEVE ME!"

She opened her purse and took out a bottle of wintergreen. "The least I can do is to take the same thing he did. I always thought that confessions were good for the soul. I read the Bible. I want to believe in your God but I can't. My god says 'an eye for an eye.' . . . Why didn't the autopsy show what he had taken?"

She was carrying a large envelope containing some

of Jimmy's things. "Will you keep these for me?"

"On condition."

"What condition?" she retorted.

"That you choose to live."

There was that cold, piercing look. "No!" she replied angrily.

She tried to open the bottle. She struggled with the lid but was unable to remove it. "Here you open it," she said.

I took the bottle and, calling her bluff, tried to unscrew the lid. It was on too tightly and besides I wasn't anxious to open it.

I turned toward her suddenly in a way that frightened her and said, "Why do you want to make me a party to your suicide? Why do you want to torment me this way?"

"All right, all right," she screamed. "How can I get rid of the thoughts?"

"You will never be rid of them. They will stay with you. You must learn to live with them."

Spitefully she threatened, "You don't believe that I will kill myself, do you?" She grabbed the bottle from me and went to the door. I sat quietly. I was pained and solemn.

She paused briefly before leaving, "I don't like to see you look that way."

I responded sarcastically, "What do you want me to do, laugh?"

Several hours later she called, "I just took the

oil of wintergreen. My stomach feels terrible. At least now I know how Jimmy felt. It's cold out here by the river and I'm so alone."

"If you want help, you know how you can get it."

"You mean I'll just have to die?"

"Yes. If you don't make an effort to get help for yourself, you'll just have to die." She hung up.

I discovered that the liquid she had with her was lethal. If she had taken it, there was a real chance that it might be fatal.

Somehow that night I didn't feel right just going home. I talked with two of my colleagues. I was wondering what should be done. Then Otto spoke. He was much more than a colleague, he was a personal friend. We had been in high school together, then our paths diverged. Now we were in the process of rediscovering each other as men and as representatives of similar professions.

"I don't think the question is what we should do, but what it will do to you if she suicides."

Many things raced through my mind. I felt helpless and alone. I wanted to drive along the river just to see if perchance I might find her.

Then, as I was leaving, I saw the lights of a car in the parking lot. As I approached the car, I saw Mary slumped over the seat, the radio was on, and there on the floor was the empty bottle.

It was snowing large, lazy flurries as Otto and

I took her to the hospital several miles away. We rushed her to the emergency room where a lavage was administered. The doctor on duty stuffed a long, thick rubber tube into her nose. He kept pushing it in further and further until I felt the horrible thing in my nose—pushing against the tender, sensitive lining. The results were soon made known. There was no trace of wintergreen in her system.

As I was leaving, she called my name. I told her I would return the following day.

The next day I entered the ward and went with her to her room. It was dimly lit—one small lamp with a dark shade casting light only in the area immediately around it. She looked haggard; her usually neatly combed hair was unkempt; her face looked old, tired, pleading, full of anguish but not total defeat.

I tried to find a beginning, "How is it going?"

She looked at me harshly, "How is it supposed to be going?"

My question seemed stupid as I heard it thrown back. There was silence.

I tried again, "I feel certain of one thing . . . you are trying hard to be honest."

"You still think I'm lying," she snapped.

"You lied about taking the wintergreen."

"I did taste it but it made my throat burn. I took a lot of pills. What's the difference?"

64

I could see that if we continued in this way, we would only become hopelessly locked in combat. "I don't want to fight with you. I didn't come here to be your accuser."

I told her that I felt we had to reach a new agreement in our relationship. I was becoming more and more convinced that my seeing her as I had the day before only made it that much more difficult for her to effect the separation. We both knew that I had been "off limits" in accepting the appointment. We drew up new "rules."

"Go ahead," she said "reject me. I've known it before. You've just sprinkled it out over a longer period of time."

"I'm not rejecting you. I do this because it seems like the only way."

She paused for some time and then looked up. "The only way I can make it, the only way I can keep the 'rules,' would be to call my sister and have her come after me. I know that if I'm anywhere near the Center, I won't be able to stay away."

Before I left I remember her saying, "How can you go on meeting with someone who hurts you so often? You must like me some to put up with me." She was trying to understand the whole experience, trying to grasp its meaning. Then, with seriousness, she remarked, "Somehow it doesn't seem fair that I can't see you—that I can't meet with you anymore." She was silent for a time, then continued,

"If I survive the winter, I would like to drop in sometime in the spring."

I agreed to grant her request, stating that if she did return in the spring, I would meet with her briefly . . . not as her doctor but as a friend.

There was something churning inside me—it was my struggle with having to have "rules." I had to know from her that she wanted me to enforce the "rules" in the interests of our mutual survival. I couldn't do it because of some theory or intellectually held knowledge.

"I hope you won't have to hate me for enforcing the rules," I said.

"No! No! I won't. I won't." She said this in a genuine way which I believed to be utterly sincere. It would be too difficult for me to enforce them alone. I needed her reassurance and support.

As I extended my hand in leaving, she broke down for a moment, "I can't keep them, I can't — it'll kill me."

"But it's killing you to see me too."

She grasped my hand tightly, looking up into my face as I stood to leave. Her eyes looked steadily into mine. She looked at me as though drinking in as much of that moment as possible—trying to implant it firmly in her mind. The grip loosened. She was still saying, "I can't, I can't."

"Please try," I said. I turned and left.

The same day I received a call from her sister in

Madison. "Mary called and asked me to come after her. Anything Mary wants Mary gets." It was clear that Mary had again deceived in order to help bring about her plan.

I discovered later that her sister did drive down and took Mary and Tommy with her to Madison. She had announced her plan to Don without permitting him a choice.

9

It is at times like these that I feel no one could **bear** all that I feel and think. He would have to turn away. He would say, "That's enough—I can't stand anymore. It drags me down. It's too depressing."

And if I can't contain it, I can at least write it down for myself—my own soul. Sometimes I wonder if it isn't, in the last analysis, only my own soul that can comfort me, can bear me, can live with me, can endure me, can give me peace and joy. Maybe this is what some people call "God."

I found myself interpreting the incident, depending on my own attitude at the time. If I feel she has victimized me, violated me in some way, then I see the evil in her and I can see it clearly. Now I know that she is capable of monstrous evil, of fantastic deceit. The last threat of suicide was for the purpose of placing herself in a position where someone else had to assume responsibility for her.

If I feel close to her, as I have on so many occasions, then I see some nobility in the incident. I understand it. She knew that she was hurting Don, Tommy, and herself immeasurably, that she was running up bills that were staggering to Don. She knew that the thoughts of Jimmy were driving her "crazy"—driving her in a way that she wasn't "good for anyone." The only way she could save Don was to make him hate her. She hoped that I would hate her too, so that I would be spared her evil. But I also knew her love. I know and have felt her warmth and tenderness, her delicate sensitivity. It is this part of her that I continued to respond to.

I tried at this time to objectify, to articulate my relationship to her as honestly as I could. I knew that I could not trust her or believe her, but I felt she was trying to be honest. I knew, too, that I had a kind of unconditional regard for her—a deep bond had been established. I kept hoping that there might be a time when I could relate to her as a friend, not in a helper-helpless relationship. I knew that I could no longer permit her to use me or rely on me. She must find her own strength apart from me. I knew that I must not under any circumstances break our new agreement and yet at times I felt that "rules" were not the final answer.

As I continued to pursue the thoughts that came into my mind, I became aware of another possible facet of myself—my own evil, my own deceitfulness. My thoughts revealed themselves in these word forms. It was as though I were talking to Mary.

I would like for you to love me because I sense that your love would be intense in its devotion and loyalty. I need radical love—the kind that few people are capable of giving. I will go to great lengths to secure that response. I will be kind, loving, forbearing, self-giving, understanding. I will overwhelm you with "love" in such a way as to cause you to feel indebted to me. If I indebt you to me, I will have the "security" of your indebtedness.

Such treachery, such insidious and pernicious deception. Your ways are at least in the open. Mine are more heinous because they are under the guise of "regard" and "therapy."

I felt, too, that perhaps Mary might have been saying something like this:

71

The "ordinary" person can't give me what I want. It must be an "extraordinary" person. He must be able to love me as I've never experienced it before—meet all my demands—then I will bask in that "love." But something else happens. The closer I come to achieving it, the more I'm able to bask in it, the more something in me is being destroyed. I'm hopelessly in debt, bound, no longer free. I've got to run, flee, or die. I've got to escape this terrible crippling, destroying "love." I need to be unshackled if I'm to live and draw on my own strength.

When you discover that "love" hurts me, that I feel so undeserving, that I can't reciprocate, that I am susceptible, then you seem to want to subject me all the more. When you discover how much I need your "love," then you overwhelm me with it as though you want to bind me to you hopelessly in guilt.

To have to look at this side of myself made me feel sick. It nauseated me. I felt "unfit," unworthy to continue meeting with people. I wanted to find a job somewhere where I wouldn't contaminate others with my honeyed poison. The only consolation, and it was slight, was that I wanted to be honest with myself—like a light shining in the dark corners of my soul; I wanted to know what was there, regardless of how ugly or hideous the contents.

o   o   o

The "rules" allowed for correspondence but no calls or meetings with me except for one in the

72

spring. The following are excerpts from a letter.

I didn't come to Madison on impulse. I had time to think it over and I did it simply because it seemed right. Right for Don, Tommy, and me. . . .

Don said that because of something I had done you told him you didn't want anything else to do with me and that you wouldn't even write to me. Maybe you did tell him that, but I am not going to believe it because if you did actually say it and if you meant it, then you will be destroying everything you, Miriam, Dick, and the others tried so hard to make me believe. If you destroy my belief in you people and the hope that maybe there really are others like you in this crazy, confused, upside-down world, then you are really just destroying me.

. . . I trusted you and the others. I believed you and I like you, not wisely but too well. I *will not* let you take that away from me. . . . I know I really went overboard as far as the way I feel about you is concerned; but can I help it if you were really and truly the first person I was ever capable of loving? There I've said it and I'm not sorry! I do love you and it hurts and feels good at the same time. . . . It's said that no matter how long and dark winter may seem, spring always follows. When the spring that I am trying so hard to bring about finally gets here, then you and the others will have the satisfaction of knowing just how very, very much you did help me. You proved to me how truly wonderful it is to just let go and really care about people; how satisfying it is to take an interest in someone or something other than yourself.

If, sometime in the future, Don is willing to have me back, maybe I can give to him what he has been waiting for for so long. I have loved Don such a very long time and there will never be anyone else. He doesn't believe this and probably you don't either, but it doesn't matter because I believe it. I told Don that as soon as I start work I'll help with the financial mess that we somehow always seem to be in. He deserves this chance to find out what he really wants. . . . As long as I was around he could never have made a decision because all I did was make him so miserable that he just didn't particularly give a damn one way or the other. My sister and her husband are starting to church with Tommy and me next Sunday. I really mean it this time because I want to accept your God. I'm intelligent enough to realize that I am my own judge and jury and if I so choose, my own executioner. . . .

I acknowledged the letter by sending her a small container of M & M candy. Once before, when she was not sure she could endure without medication, I had given her a vial of M & M's. She was quick to catch the message, "How many am I supposed to take?"

"Never more than 15 at any one time." We both had laughed.

One day shortly before spring, Miriam handed me the same vial filled with extra large M & M's. "Mary said to tell you that these *have nuts.*"

74

10

Then, the arrival of spring and with it this letter:

You promised me that I wouldn't become a puppet. When I goofed and did exactly what you said I wouldn't do, you tried so terribly hard to help me break away. I wasn't ready and because I wasn't ready, I certainly wasn't ready or willing to try. I really believe that every puppet deserves the opportunity to cut his or her own strings. I pushed you in a corner and you came out fighting with "rules." Then I was in a corner. I'm getting out simply by "putting into practice what you all preached." One thing keeps fighting me back: the memory I have of the way you looked the last two times I saw you. When that picture pops in view, I can't respect or even like me. Only I know for sure how much I have really changed. Please let me give you the satisfaction of knowing too. Don said that you didn't give him the things you have of mine; so I would like to get them and say good-bye as it should be said. I know, without a doubt, that I am ready now. If you truly meant all the things you've said, it will mean as much to you as it will to me to replace that awful memory with a smile. . . . Please let me have my self-respect back so I can think of you without feeling ashamed.

In another excerpt from the same letter, Mary continued:

Too, I keep thinking about what someone said or I read it or something, about faith, spiritual love, knowledge, all those things: "You don't believe it; you feel it." I like that.

. . . By the way, Saturday, a week ago, Don and I were going home from work (overtime no less!) and we were listening to the radio. "Claude Eatherly was arrested again for robbing a store where he was well known. He used a toy pistol, then went home and waited for the police. . . ."

Somehow I didn't want to believe that this was

76

another "trick," another manifestation of her clever-
ness and deception, but these thoughts forced themselves upon me. I knew that it was really within the
"rules" and yet my own disbelief and distrust gnaw-
ed within. On the other hand, I felt that she was
trying to be honest and that even if only part of
the letter were true, perhaps I could meet with her
for the purpose of returning the necklace and rings.

I left the following message with the secretary in
the event Mary called for an appointment:

"He will have the things ready for you this Friday, Good Friday, and he would like to meet with
you briefly at 4:30 for the purpose mentioned in
your letter."

As I pondered the approaching meeting, I wanted
somehow to convey to her the broader dimensions of
our experience and relationship. She had said to keep
the items "until I am worthy of them." I took
seriously the meaning that the return of the items
might have for her. There was so much that I
wanted to say but felt that words alone could not
convey it fully.

I felt nervous when she arrived and saw her own
nervousness as well. I did not usher her to my office
but instead led the way to the small chapel. I opened the door and we went inside.

I had placed on the altar a wooden man and
woman with strings attached, a scissors, the empty
bottle which had contained the lethal liquid, an-

other bottle containing M & M's, and lastly, the necklace with the cross and the two small gold rings.

As we entered the chapel, she looked at me in a frightened way and pulled back. "It's all right," I said. She looked dazed. I repeated the same words. "It's all right. I've placed the items on the altar."

Slowly she drew near. I didn't understand her expression. I felt I saw fear, distrust, and surprise.

She began reading the notes that I had attached to each of the symbols.

LOVE AND SEVERED CORDS

These cords can only be
Severed as both parties are
Ready.

The readiness is possible
Only because of freely
Given—not demanded—
Trust, honesty, faith,
Hope, and love.

These are not mere words to be
"Believed" because someone else
Said so. . . .

As you have said, "You feel it"
And know . . .
And know that the other
KNOWS.

To me, in this, there is something
Sacred and deeply religious.

SCISSORS ARE FOR CUTTING

These scissors are for cutting.
Cutting involves pain,
And yet, True Love frees, does
Not bind, has no strings, does
Not cling, nor try to possess.

Neither does it require "rules."

It rejoices in the happiness of
Others and participates in their
Suffering.

And if you be free,

You can—in love—

Free others to be.

Like ripples from a stone
Cast into the water,
He who is not afraid to risk
Loving another may find ever
Widening circles of
Love and Communion.

She picked up the scissors and held them in her hand.

"Should I just go ahead and cut them?"

"Yes."

She turned back toward the altar. "All of them?"

She cut them one by one and then hesitated on the last. She was trembling. She took the scissors in both hands and cut the last one.

DEATH

This bottle symbolizes the
Reality of
Death.
It is the story of suffering
And the
Cross.
Death is the final separation,
The final severance.

If a person knows in his soul
What it is to LIVE AND LOVE,
Then death is not to be feared,
For it is the natural
Culmination
of
LIFE.

She looked back and smiled as she came to the
bottle of M & M's. We exchanged light comments
which broke the tenseness of those few moments.

LIFE

This bottle (of M & M's *with nuts*)
Symbolizes the reality of
Growth
and
Life,
of
New Life.

This is the story of Spring,
Of Easter,
Of This Day.

These rings are symbols of your relationship
To the family,
To Jimmy, to Tommy, and to Don
And to the
Family of Man.

The necklace with the silver cross embraced this note:

A symbol of commitment and dedication
To your own personal values.
May you be loyal to what you hold dear
And so live your life as to fulfill that
Which is uniquely

YOU.

Suddenly she seemed in a great hurry to leave. "May I have what you wrote?"

"Of course."

She quickly gathered up the items with the notes and started for the door.

"I would like to see the necklace on," I said, holding out my hand.

She understood. She handed the necklace to me . . . then turned and stood in front of the altar. I placed the small silver cross about her neck . . . and felt with my whole being the profound depth and exquisite beauty of that moment.

As she left, I thought I saw pain in her face as though she were fighting to hold back a flood of emotions.

o   o   o

Alone, behind the closed door of my office, I pondered the experience, fearing that it had overwhelmed her.

Why did I have to make such a "big thing" of it? I really knew why. Because to me, it was a "big thing."

From somewhere . . . deep within each of us . . . a new spring was born.

THE AUTHOR

Leonard Smucker lives with his wife, Lois, and their four sons in a woods near Elkhart, Indiana, where he enjoys woodcarving, growing bonsai, and playing guitar.

He is recipient of a B.A. degree from Bluffton College, Ohio; a B.D. degree from Bethany Seminary, Chicago; and a Ph.D. from the University of Southern California in 1959. Under a post-doctoral fellowship, he served his internship in psychotherapy at the Merill Palmer Institute, Detroit. For the past four years, he has been associated with the Oaklawn Psychiatric Center, Elkhart, as clinical psychologist.